One Morning—

One

Rebecca Wolff

Wave Books Seattle & New York

Morning—

Published by Wave Books

www.wavepoetry.com

Copyright © 2015 by Rebecca Wolff

Wave Books titles are distributed to the trade by

Consortium Book Sales and Distribution

Phone: 800-283-3572 / SAN 631-760x

Library of Congress Cataloging-in-Publication Data

Wolff, Rebecca, 1967–

[Poems. Selections]

One morning— / Rebecca Wolff. — First edition.

pages ; cm

ISBN 978-1-940696-12-6 (hardcover) —

ISBN 978-1-940696-13-3 (softcover)

I. Title.

PS3623.O56A6 2015

811'.6—dc23

2014042627

Designed and composed by Quemadura

Printed in the United States of America

9 8 7 6 5 4 3 2 1

First Edition

Wave Books 051

3

4

Margot

1

Arcadia (et in . . . est)

Do (fever) dreams, in fever,
teach any lesser
lesson

Traveller,
Your journey has been long

and sectional.

Because the thought is discontinuous
does not make it therefore . . .

unshapely

By night everything seems impossible

By day, by extension, everything: possible

"as water is to oil,
and oil is to water,
for that matter"

Set yourself a project

To think of another

for the first time

(pause for reflection)

"as water is to oil,
and oil is to water,
for that matter"

By night everything seems impossible

By day, by extension, everything: possible

Because the thought is discontinuous
does not make it therefore . . .

unshapely

Traveller,
Your journey has been long

and sectional.

Do (fever) dreams, in fever,
teach any lesser
lesson

One morning—

I woke up—
baked him
a bannock

The Germans had arrived
bright and early
in their Fascism

to point out
a spot on the Table,
a spot of water (WaterSpot) on the Veneer.

A German, bright, almost glowing
too bright to look at
          directly

one must look to the
          left

and the right of him,
a capitalized proper noun

A German steps from behind the Tree

The Reductions

Let's go out and buy something. In the sun.

No, let's stay home and make something, the sun floods the room. It could be green, on paper. It could be money. That's the way to create new matter.

That's how I detach boats from moorings—my boat, my mooring—
     the harbor
shallow in low tide

skiff propelled over buffeting sand flats on

sheer
puissance.

Seeming inevitability

I love how
you o'ershadow me

frontal lobe
        favoritism.

Did she say
"vomiting out the demon
of handwriting analysis"?
live on national broadcast radio not even

two days after George Carlin's untimely death?

Retreat from Likeness

vacation library, spring break,
Ocracoke Island, 2009

360 degrees around

my head

O

Design This Day
Great Historic Places
Life's Picture History

of Western Man

Life's Picture History

of World War II

One Hundred Master Drawings
The Early Work
The Later Work
Re-Purposes of Art and

Civilization

the Early
the Doric

Visual Experience

Arts and Cultures
                of Man
the Voices of Silence
Encyclopedia of
                the Early
Masters of
        Design Continuum
The Art of
        Natural Healing
Art of This Century
Architecture of
        America
        Drawing
Basic Color
Masters of
                the Modern World
        and Reality (Imagination)

The Language of (Art)
Understanding (the Arts)

Ekphrastic

there are some things up there
uptown

I want to see

I want to see   I'm going to look at that and see

I want to go up and see

that show. That show

I went to see, I went to see.

There are some things up
there   uptown

I want to

look at that and see. I'm going to see

what I look. What I look at, when I look, vessel,

I stood to see. I went to stand to look

to see. Venturing further I went outside myself to look
at that wall. It fed! There was a box inside that was not blank, I saw it.
It was really different from an aura, the thing had

colors, the thing was talking

to itself. And spoke

to me, not incidentally.

From Where
I'm Situated

Interspecies:
me and future
me, me and me
in the past. "You
smell like summer,"

he said, near
enough, but I missed
the hint. Low

self

esteem.
Now
I
could kick

myself.
Why

do we privilege
the aesthetic
object?

Ecco Ekphrastic

"I Stood in Front of It"
—Helen Frankenthaler—

"for a very long time"

that was not the extent
though there's plenty novelty
in the activity

for me
est-elle homme ou femme?

the big questions
inquiry

3-D glasses help—has to gain
dimensionality
somehow.

And he would not shut up
or step aside

to allow a clear view-
finder. It makes me feel like
reading.

It cleared that space
for reading. (Not the placard.) I cannot be left alone

in the encounter
with the valued object. Thank you

again New

York City for your cultural

institutions they are the ONLY

redeeming . . . Ekphrasitic. Salvatore

Del Deo, *Big Blue and Becalmed,* taking
as your subject
folly the subject

of boats ships lights and light
—make it too real
and I won't see it

Look at the paint
Look at the paint
Look at the paint it's

dark blue it's
bright blue

Stockholder

This view of the mountain puts me in mind
of another view, a different mountain.

Recollection, a cement plant, voyage
alone in the misty isles

coast of Scotland, an error.
Representation of solitude,

gratuitous.

This view of the mountain once put me in mind
of a different view, another mountain. I rose up its side

a shade up a glade

a glen in a vale

mist in a fog

descent all but

forgotten.
Misremembered.

That was ten years ago.
That was ages

behind us

in front of us now
a spectacle

The mountain!
A different mountain.

How can I buy

a piece of it.

2

Let's consider this a

rich
terrain, a gold mine or a mine
for gems or jewels in rough
condition

deportment
comportment

A sinkhole or a rockpool

an infinite

it is my decision
to do so
and thereby live
most fully
forever

in my special
dimension

Palisades

Interred in region

nothing super global in this locale

where I live, where I
bought—

what would I tell you about it if I could?

What I see when I go up
what I see when I go down

the right hand side
left hand
shudder and roll of conveyance

that's just locked in motion.
That's just the place inside.

Some poets find their place
in place

and naming it seems venturesome
that seems to me a tiresome—

and I wish no longer—.

I stand
on reeds or rocks until

they lose their root in soil or sky around—

Never
Never say

Get me out of here.

How Spooky Is It

Standing on a rutty road
midwinter thaw

I recall once being told
"You're in a rut"—

How spooky it is even now
to pull anything out of the water

an old TV set
the cord a drag

Presumably it is all for the best

We are the quietest neighbors
anyone on the planet

could ask for
Better than fun

is quiet

anyone could ask for

Man Tits

Look at that pair,

on the one over there.
He's young, skinny, low
muscle tone, poor, white, under-
educated . . . gazing
down
on a
path

in the little patch
of yard in front of his
unfavorably situated
rental where he stands, hands
on hips, mutable, conceivable
speculation on the next weekend
chore.

But his tits are the good
kind: fat, conical, pale against
the brown of his wife-beater tan,
nipples slightly shiny,
areolate. Bouncy, native tits

like the ones you came to see.

Tuck In, Vermont

local
obits

over buffet

You don't know where I am

reading material
orbiting
Middle-

bury

paid notices

You truly were the best husband a woman could ever ask
for as well as my soul mate, best friend, and hero. I am so

thankful for every moment we spent together. The thought
of living the rest of my life without you seems unbearably
lonely and scary "at times."

No one needs
adjectives

I choke up

patronage

Buncha Corporate Trash

hanging on a stoop

on the block where I grew up.
My choice

to make a shape.

They are in full view looking like

portraiture
tacky

fuckn giant black vehicular
weekender crammed with
duffels of product, weary

man retrieving
my car
secreted

down deep
in the garage
across the street
has apologized for having been asleep

when I knocked on his plexiglass. "Sorry," he says,

"it's boring."

Here I am the apologizer.

Bumper Sticker

Careening over the
highway in
my lightweight
Japanese
Death Star
buffeted by the great and powerful
winds

icy winds
of winter warming
cold air with hot air
under it

accordion pleats
of natural disaster
my disaster

in the past if you were to say to me

or to rage at me
in a poem
about America I would charge you
a great failure

to even use the word. It is
banality
this land is suffering because poets—

their great cohort—

I look twice
to save lives.

Mad as Hell/Not Going to Take It

When they tapered off my meds
           (no "they")
began to feel it

they say depression is anger
misspent
           (no "they" anywhere)

tapered off my meds unsupervised

food tastes larger
loins activate
crystal reformation

into pronoun conversion

was elected to become
accounted for

raised my hands into
criminalized

feeling politicized
finally

long sigh.

feeling it at the gas pump
fumes unchained

—I will report you—

squad car drove up
my tailpipe

called my friend
in

to see what he could do for us.

Abs

Ulrike Meinhof
      Meinhof
      Meinhof

Maddening.

20 reps
in descending order
of

auditory
processing
disorder

of steel

of magical thinking:

If I blow up that statehouse

it is a block away from my house.

It's all about her.

She's just like me.

Short Sight

Short in sight   in stature   radio personality

shortsighted   to caricature one's self—never do that. *Never* let anyone
make you do that to yourself.

Shortsighted, a special election on the 31st of the month of March

the cryptic, out of fashion
the Coptic, obsolete

short first three months in office shortsightedness

the degraded life of the average "American"
small town in Ohio
motorized barstool races

Shortsightedness of exemplary—
of plenary—

To close the shop on Sundays
when we might make a purchase—

recriminations

necessary to suppress

the urge
to recriminate

I'm in the wrong business

What, you don't want my business?

I approach a purchase

adore my children—
back away—
that they revere ugliness

the rainbow bag
that holds a smaller
rainbow bag

I just forgot! (isn't
that a scream)
to stand outside

the vault of apt

comparison.

Greed You Cannot Think About
(Sneaking Sally through the Alley)

a roster of big properties
the same few garments
     over and over
each day—classy
old bohemian in her

sandals in December
headed straight for your pinched
receptors like a Hummer on ped
mall
I've decided to

reject consumer culture!
The surge of power I only (feel)
when someone's buying
it.

The light tenor of *lunch*,
of *drinks*, of *dinner*

I want the talk,
and he wants to fuck me

with his fake dick,

unmediated—
or mediated by dream
eating chicken close

to the mouth, the deep-fried
head of legend.

In the affirmative
a fake penis
on a real man

fucked and fucking at the same
time
fairly enflamed

the raucous
fake penis
a real man
the affirmative

Antiques Roadshow (Nounz 2 Verbz)

drama drama
drama drama
drama drama the

things
find their way
into pop
entertainment: Can it truly be that

a higher culture . . . Grandma's

Navajo blanket rape pillage? You're

weeping 30,000
dollars. Angel
Moroni risen a real

relic. Word reaches back
to early Victorians: Those young Americans

are Morons! It's a

hodge podge
hodge podge
hodge podge. Now I have to go

memorabilia Devo.

Use Objects: Boise Art Museum 2009

I just want to touch everything
hanging from the walls and the ceiling

I've never felt this way before . . . *Ruth Duckworth*—is she
truly still living?
The card says so. What do I want to look at

a bunch of quilts hanging on the wall for? I am almost done

with this guileless pose
exhaust one's self in several poses
currently standing and looking
my ass off

at doll quilts 1863
            in a glass box
everything darker
just the general tenor of life
                     —darker

the fabrics, candlelight, eyes

shut at sundown
"Sunshine and Shadow pattern"
made with tiny stitches a whole lot of sense

Unbelievable—
that human intelligence—
now so dulled—
could have flamed

so bright as to stitch this square
with a lady's fan

a velvet boot
tilted teacup.

And then I went to see *Bright Star*

and wept more in the dark for that recaptured
affect

peering at poems,
by candlelight, when night
was dark.

GDP

We don't need the shit you're making
                (factory smokestack)
                (blackening plume)

Do you need the shit I'm making?

I am not in the mood for the shit you're
making (museum) and the mood
art puts me in

and the profanity
(that) issuance
      that issueth
        therefore

      production =
    comeuppance

Applies to Apple

for Bob Ajar and Roy Kortick

onion in her
cynicism

peel away another layer of

apple

the weakest
link

rolls down the hill

far from the tree away

and bruised
and rotten amongst

a bunch

applies to

human

applies

to endeavor

the ruminant

remainder goats

fed on fallen

apples make flesh
make apple milk
apple-goat-meat
in apple-goat-milk

aged
and resplendent with

spores
and cultivars

age-old

endeavor of

humans on a weekend
visit other
humans with their animals

seeding

(the) human web
(I've been in it so long)

press of bodies

to draw away and press

on other areas

of apples
of need
of desire
to move away

from the city famously

and even farther away

Fronting

I front
because I can

I front because
I care: the secret to fronting

you must never stop
to think gleaming

rows
pristine abundance

saucy daughter
of the devil, *fra diavolo*

I'm not using metaphor:
I can't get over how much I love

this product design,
and the conceit of the product

(which is delicious, btw):
SuperFruits, from disparate continents.

That impulse to make things look pretty
and sell more

in the agrarian landscape
unprecedented

divisions of labor—friendly old hippies
unfriendly young hippies—I feed six people

and then I stop.
That soup sells

and this soup obviously doesn't sell as much.
And I trust people

to make good choices
so I don't have to impale them

on the tines of my pitchfork. Or otherwise

govern them. Why do you need so much
government, if you don't like government why

do you insist upon making
these bad choices.

The Ungovernable

One thing I'm not doing in my poems: reporting
on anything that really happened.

When I say I'm from New York, Glaswegians say, "Oh, I love Woody
Allen." They cannot construe how large a state can be. I just happen to
actually be from Manhattan.

How impractical, to imagine that a structure like a government would be
responsive to the needs of such a lot of people. Held like in a holding pen.

In the early 1990s I saw a yellow Indian drunk in a tattoo parlor in
Seattle. He literally said he could literally see right through me. If he said
it figuratively I took it literally.

A lot of people in America do not want regulation from the government.
In principle: our forefathers, our persecution. Ideally we wouldn't need
industries and individual actions to be regulated. We wouldn't even need
laws.

People, including people who run corporations or work for them, would just behave responsibly. Corporations would take the responsibility of personhood seriously.

My mother cannot be trusted to restrict me from buying R-rated videogames at the porn store.

My mother struggled to love me—the firstborn had been so tractable—she still struggles to love me—can she be commanded to love me? Now I see what those commandments are about. There must be a God.

Objectively we could expect that our family members would go out of their way to behave toward us with extra care, concern, and with love.

Sometimes there is a harsh disjunction between what objective perception would suggest to us we might expect and what really takes place, or "occurs," within the framework of what we call "our lives."

I really saw the other day for the first time that my mother did not naturally take to me—I am not much like her. It would take an effort for her to understand what matters to me. (Her love will come around.)

My own daughter is quite different from me—I think—it's hard to tell, she is only five years old. But she looks different—takes after her father, as I took after mine—and so far her concerns are not my own. She loves pink. I hate pink. (My love moves faster.)

Where would that moral activity come from, to behave responsibly toward others? Not to overcharge, not to seek loopholes, not to dominate, not to oppress. Does anyone consciously oppress? I guess some spousal abuse comes from the pure urge to dominate, and the ire that results when that domination is resisted, or thwarted . . .

But is it a pure urge or is it coming from an inscribed narrative of gendered hierarchy? Like a man wearing a wife-beater has been told too many times that his wife is supposed to listen to him and obey him. Now if he can be told by the government that "My Strength Is Not for Hurting," a local billboard campaign, maybe that will ring in his ears when he lifts his fist.

If the government doesn't do it, who will do it? The church used to do it, and still does. The one time I went to church, with my mother, in Tennessee, when we were at a family reunion and the whole family had certain activities, and one of them was "church on Sunday," I was brought to tears by the simple goodness of the message that the pastor, or reverend —minister?—this was a Methodist church—was preaching. It was Father's Day, actually, and he talked about how fathers ought to make sure to spend time with their kids. Turn off the TV, he said, and spend some time with your kids.

I was crying because I am not used to an experience of shared instruction in goodness. It was very moving to be in a room with real people all receiving the same instruction.

3

The Curious Life
and Mysterious Death
of Peter J. Perry

At the end

he was tilted that he might
remain in sleep.
If he woke he would know
just how bad
things were, would cough and dislodge
the intubation tube. A certainty. Fluids
in, fluids
out. Tilted his head
below his heart, all the rest
he never sought pooled
in the sunken gates
of his eyes, the
grate of his jaw.

Points of sophistication

sophistry
the bony knobs of his arthritic
knuckles. His Adam's apple
his lungs filled up

he never woke up.

*

Between the misery of the end
and the glory of beginning

all the glowing love made flesh

time collapses
disgorging banalities.
Certain are goldmines
certain are minefields
Time, mind, brain: "collapses."

The body functions
that much his sister knows
but the ties between the mind
and it
she will not recognize. He's dead; she's eating

his leftover painkillers to kill
the pain of
spasms

free-floating sadness
putting Bozo to sleep. The dog would not eat. In his obituary,
in a town paper he never knew,
a middle initial he always used. His daddy's
name was Jennings, his middle name was
Jennings. It's irritating when folks
don't spell it out. That's my hidden voice speaking. If I did not speak

you would have to assume I was the one
that killed him.

   *

To move through the death back
alive

a green and gold brightness segmented in the screen
door's squares, stitched with glue
where the dog poked through, his loyal
claws. Peter sitting there
day after day, unbelievable what a being

can come to. Coke Rewards in the drawer, he would
cash them in at the store but
he can't get there, can't get anywhere. Twelve
years ago or so a massive stroke, *suffered*
it, they say, routinely. The things we say routinely, we say "we,"
    routinely. I

dive for these worn phrases, and suddenly
it's all about me again. It's not all about me.

Peter J. Perry

was born in West Tennessee. No. He lived in West Tennessee. Peter J.
    Perry

was born

in the south of France, to Pat, a motherless drunk from Buffalo, escaped
    the convent, Jennings
a philandering newspaperman, fled Nashville to be Hemingway
already. Writing stories for the rags

on hounds and fishes. Two escapees, really. Their stories are so much
richer for the times they lived in allowed it.

*

Peter's time allowed that he die with the television on in his hospital
room as it had been on around the clock for twelve years as he sat, bony
knees and elbows, bony ass, on a malmy couch in a corner of a living
room overrun by kittens and wild dogs and mice. The kittens ate the
mice and the dogs ate the kittens, right in front of his eyes. He had a
sweetness, Pete. Sweet on the animals, so he wanted them near, but hard
so that he could bear it when they went and did their tricks: Getting hit
by cars in front of the house, at the far end of the lawn, Pete sitting in his
wheelchair on the rotting porch. Pissing in a corner of the room where
Pete kept all the important things, his genealogical charts and the albums
of photos of Pat and Pop, a shot
of the two of them on bicycles in the Sahara. It is said they bicycled across
the Sahara Desert.

Who says it?
It is not important that you be convinced of Pete's importance. What
follows is family history, in my voice the way I learned it.

Peter was not loved properly by his mother. Pat was tall, bony, elegant,
mannish, with a small squared-off mouth, a cigarette jammed in it. A
proud nose, a high brow, thin, lank hair, small eyes, long face, the bones
of her cheeks high and prominent. You think, "supermodel." She did do

some modeling for sculptors and photographers. Big hands, big feet. She posed as a diver, and the Jantzen swimming suit company used her bowed form for its logo, a Deco figure. Then she was drunk and dove off a bridge and hit her chest on a log in the river and tore the tissue of her breasts. There was some surgical repair. In France.

Peter was not loved properly by his mother; she did not take care of him. He played by himself on the beach down at the bottom of France, tall cliffs behind him, speaking both languages, and felt lost. He did not know where she was and she allowed him to search for her. She infused him singly with her own desires and set him on a path down which he loped. Eight abortions between his birth and that of his sister, Pamela. Pop could not, or would not, take certain measures. There was something about Pop like a stud horse, something like a prize bull, though he was not a large man, very dapper, like a squinty Clark Gable. George Clooneyish. Maybe they were "crazy about each other," maybe the love they felt transmuted into flesh, over and over again, and had to be removed surgically.

These are the people who made these people. These are the true stories of their lives, though I am telling them. This is why soap opera is important to my friends. What else is so real: video art? Documentation of a moment, elderly man breathing into a mirror, yes, but it neglects the span, the span of years, about which I am aching, alive with mortality. It takes years to watch a whole life pass. Days of our lives.

So now when he dies, can you feel it? You can't feel it, and when I say it it's just the word, and you feel nothing but informed.

Every time I feel it again I'll come back to this page for you.

*

Three points
Three reasons
Three rules

Aggregate of the diameter, the reasons he lived, the reasons he died, the rules by which he lived, the rules by which he died, the point of talking about it now he's dead. Deterioration of his majesty, his manhood. He was a tall, sexy man, a deep rich voice on a tall, skinny man, not overly nice, long arms and legs, lean, naked ladies tattooed on his forearms. He made them dance by twirling his wrists, and in the first years after the stroke you could still feel his strength and his aggression even in his disability. At first he wanted to speak, and he tried to be understood, with the half of his face that worked. But over the years he lost the power, or he lost the desire, to be understood. Over the years of his abrupt then gradual decline his patience for visitors grew shorter and shorter. A side effect of the stroke was a mildness, an acceptance, a resignation even, and he lived for twelve years in an isolation and inactivity that would have made any other man cry out. It is possible that he did cry out, sometimes, alone in that old farmhouse in West Tennessee, on a country road bordering cotton fields and wild dogs, tenant farmers dropping by once a week or so to check on him, replenish his stores of buttermilk and TV dinners, big pint mug of flat Coke he kept on the Plexiglas-topped coffee table next to the couch on which he sat all day long, day in and day out, and lay down on to sleep when the night grew deep enough that he could give up. He watched television all day long, and all night long. I don't know what he thought about; I don't know what anyone thinks about. His thinking must have had a flatness to it even before the stroke. He kept a little calendar, and in it he wrote the anniversaries of his parents' deaths, his own birthday, doctors' appointments, when the cats kitted and the dogs pupped, noted his sister's quarterly visits.

When Pam came she brought her haircutting scissors, trimmed his beard and the lank, iron-grey hairs of his head. He wore a black Air Force cap every day, and as best she could she would free it of the oils of his hair. She got him onto his plastic chair in the shower, washed him. Scraped the cat shit off the floorboards, vacuumed the rugs, hired a man to patch the porch where it was rotting. Hired another to mow the lawn, another to come by for emergencies, like the time the pipes froze. For twelve years every three months, shoring up his attenuated life in the old farmhouse in which their father had been born, and where they played as kids.

And what did she get out of it?

And did they converse, while she restored order? It was not in their nature to converse. Muted by mother? It was in Pete's nature to tell stories, discomfiting stories, about hurricanes and suicides, about family dementia, stories of a peculiar grisly glory. But now he could not get far enough in his sentences: would close his mouth on the gobstopping word and wave his one good hand, long, bony, in front of his own face, like shooing off a lazy fly, a perfunctory rejection, a perfect dismissal—say "F'get it." And she was not a talker. She came to the farmhouse so that she could not talk to her brother.

*

Unbelievable what a being

*

a stagehand
summer stock
prop handler
in his youth
he was loved
by women but he did not
love them, it seems. There was no love or talk of love.

He married one wealthy woman, recent divorcée, a new mother
of a baby boy named Mikey. Complicated situation. She was not simply
wealthy, she was an heiress, they lived in bohemian
grandeur in Patchin Place.

Who else lived there?

e.e. cummings lived there, a shady doorway. Theodore Dreiser lived
there. John Reed lived there. I think

Dawn Powell may have lived there, for a time. Deborah
paid for Pete, bought him

an airplane, a boat, Amagansett
estate where they kept thirty-six cats. Pete
helped with the boy, loved the boy, boy loved him,
when Deborah threw Pete out he took
Mikey, flew off to Big Pine Key in his
little plane. Kept him there for weeks,

returned without a fight. What's best for the boy. Mikey
has been alerted of his death. Mikey sought him out once, grown man,
    light beard,
flying in from San Francisco to visit
the eviscerated man, bony and dehydrated in St. Croix. They spent a day
fishing and drinking, Mikey

flew back home, no one came
back. It's astonishing how people

will abandon
will neglect to
will abstain
will restrict
will refrain from
will hold themselves away
will deny Pete

*

Pat and Pop
Pop and Pat
At the end
together.

Pat o'ershadowed
her children. All three of them in Greenwich Village
in shared apartments, swapping beds and walls and jobs
sometimes. They had all fled Tennessee.

Later on, when her children wed
and began to breed Pat fled
to Athens—seat of civilization? Or maybe
that's Israel—or Baghdad. And then

she lived awhile and then

and then
and then
and then
and then
and
and
and
and
and
and
and
and
when she began to die
she began to die
she began

dying
dying dying
dying
dying dying
dying
dying dying
dying

dying dying
dying
dying dying parts of her body

failing: retina, kidney, heart, lung. All the systems abused
with drink and smoke
in final rebellion
deported (can you believe that? An old dying woman)

ejected. Pam picked her up at the airport
in an ambulance. To St. Vincent's, where
others have died (Edna Millay's named after it for
the sanctuary *her* uncle
received)
and when it was clear
she was dying

sent on back to Nashville
to die at home with her husband with whom
she had not lived for twenty-odd years. But apparently

they'd always loved each other. Wrote letters. Thought of one
another constantly. Pat didn't

want to live in Tennessee.
But she died there.

*

The pint mug was from TGI Fridays.
Pete was a bouncer for five years or so while
Pop was ill. Pete set himself up
in his old room upstairs, piles of porn all around
the bed, worked in his spare
time on an Austin-Healey Mark III up on blocks in the yard. Haverford,
sounds like a manor house. A small stone house with a coolness, a
    dimness, a breakfast
nook where Pop sang Little Boy Blue and other rather mournful songs.
    He had Parkinson's, and it took him a long time to die. Surrounded
    in his den
by young women. One buxom red-haired nurse took up with Pete
and kept up with him for a while, even after Pop died, until Pete

bought a houseboat in St. Croix. And then he lived there till
the hurricane took everything. He had no insurance, and he came back
to stay at the farm, to fix things up. Built a woodshop in the back, started
fixing things up. Fixed things up, built shelves for his records and books,
fixed up a cat door on the back so the cats could come and go. Pruned the
trees, hung his tools on hooks, mowed the lawn, one day woke up on the
floor and could not speak, could not use his arm or leg, dragged himself
across the floor to the phone and called my mom.

No relation.

*

Who will remember Peter J. Perry

his nonrepresentative life, his pointless. ineluctable, singular death?

There is no reason that he must be remembered.
Everyone deserves to be remembered?
For the extraordinary things he did.
For his ashes.

Memory: A memoir. A memorial. In memoriam. For the ages. His ashes

disseminated. It is

my love that draws him out. It is my love
you must contend with.

4

Admit No Impediment

I'm going to get up from the table
and go to the bathroom

When I get back,
if your napkin has moved
from the left side of your plate
to the right, I'll
know you want to.

There will be no need to speak.
Or, wait a minute,
maybe it should be if your napkin
hasn't moved.

I want to make this
as easy for you
as I can.

A million metaphors

has to feel strong

I use my pussy
correctly
a compass

your magnetic head
lodestone—directive

put my eyes
inside your eyes

my head
inside your head

bird
flown heartless for a minute

find myself
there I am

facedown
heart shaped

all by myself I have to feel

no pressure
no future

your cock
in my throat
finger
up your ass

put pressure inside there

midwifing
the shit out of
this morning

Poor Mr. Rochester

synesthete

with his dark eye
(ruined, blind)

his insatiable eye for

me and only me
he's only

learning it now

a found paperback, smells
of ritual

instruction, promise
of the most pungent magic

marker in the world against

his cock, everything

against his one-eyed
smoldering

Master Mind

If you say put your ass right here
I'm going to put my ass

right here plush

fuck

blue

interior

light's really good
bright snow

on the trees all around
dark sky

packed with more
stationery

but you're moving
I am not

losing myself
assent

assent
assent

colored pegs in order
what order
what color

a blind like a raptor

bird blind like a bird
in a blind
bloody wet

spot live
in it

Church on the Hill

If you love two people at the same time, choose the second one. Because if you truly loved the first one, you wouldn't love another. There are four questions of value in life . . . What is sacred? Of what is the spirit made? What is worth living for, and what is worth dying for? The answer to each is the same. Only love. —JOHNNY DEPP

It's as though I thought that I could understand every side
from the outside

even the side blind

bring intelligence to bear on
duplication

manufacture
of understanding

you came to it

unrigorous voice in the spring

time of our underground
natural—the word is *trickling*

++

I *was* blind

now I *do* see

occlusion up ahead   top of the hill
a cultlike
churchgoing

lesson in book-
learning

daughters with lots of things to do besides

all the things I did

and mirror-daughter sleeping,
sick-day,
on the floor in the kitchen I cooked

soup.

This never would have happened in ménage
a ménage that prevents is a ménage that

convent

or monastery on top of the hill a mound of men
underhill, refutation

angling a steep
with hidden structure

self-actualization maybe
never would have happened

when I come down off this hilltop
over the other side of the hill

it will all be over

you won't love me   and I won't
love you   that mandate absconded which called us

up the hill

+ + +

Don't leave the church out-

side, the churchyard is a graveyard as exposed as a hill-

top when we reach it, we never reach it because we

pass it

land on a bed and are moronic to-
gether

"there's a reason it's called

church on the hill"

The Things That I Do

that give me away
everyone can see it

but no one will tell me
what it looks like

You could say I
act unconscious

or you could say I appear
to be following

the advice of spirit
guides

either way

around the corner
I am coming around the corner

a visibility
blindsided

the things that I do
a shame and a
torment

the things that I do
are proud and contented. And no one

knows which, and everyone

loves me just the same, shit
on my face, honey

in my mouth.

What happened

the pun of "what happened?" and "what happened." I was going to make
    something out of it.

You and I

we never get a chance to get
our stories straight.

if something bad happens
it was bad
that it happened

and there's the spot I drooled
on the floor
mouth open to the floor finally

"I loved him—
he loved me—"
symphonic

chamber we first made love in I drive by
frequently

consider the wisdom of doing
myself in,

we never get a chance to do
anything more than once

doing myself

in there

verily compose the note
I left:

here is where my life began
here is where I'll end it.

I'm giving him too much power over me,
don't you think?

But oh I should not have invited him to haunt me.
But oh I invited him to haunt me.

Supply

survive
maintain enduring endless welcoming visitation

I do today forever.

My fair beauty recalls him.

My spitting image recalls him. Sinewed thighs

barren ribcage recall him. Eyes
inside my eyes.

Everpresence

The point about Heathcliff's impersonality or non-humanness
has been made repeatedly by critics. According to Chase,
both Emily and Charlotte Brontë suffered from a failure in
nerve; in different ways, both backed off from uniting their
heroines and their demonic lovers. —academic.brooklyn.cuny
.edu/english/melani/novel_19c/wuthering/sex.html

fallacy of affinity
heathcliff and cathy

poor stringent cathy whose sex is in her purse
she thinks she's so hot
but she ain't—heathcliff would be hot
with her body on the plane
but she will not allow it, insists on their astral

fuck
on the moor
on the afterlife.

discomfort on the rocks of the afterlife.

fallacy of conjuring one whose beckoned, disagreeable, unwilling phantasm replies: "I am not anywhere where I am not. Send me back to the hell of my own life in which you do not imagine me. That is where I am and you can't see me there, because there is where I really am. And you can't see me. Because you are not there with me. Forever after."

Parkeresque

I'd like a
lidless

Vicodin.
Oblivion.

Countless
sensation of him

leaving the room.
Come back soon.

It occurred to me
fait accompli

Clinamen.
Phantom limb.

Black cat sleeping
(you used to be

next to me)
next to me

dreams our lost
telepathy.

Let Your Secrets Die with Me

Coming flying around the corner as I do my only wish

is just to see you. Your head your face attached. Narrow

and finessed—I only wish

just to see you. This is all that is left. And yet, and yes, that's total, what's
    broke, what is sorrow. What I learned

now to arrive: booming into sound, taking my only name
back from the crowd. You never spoke to me of

nothing but love, you never always said the things it made a template. I have

both the single and the double and the minor in my rucksack. I have
    everything
that's yours and all the things you never gave me. I have gone

another round the corner left here. There is a place you left me.

Come now to the hollow derivation of your names. Egress further
complication to the name. You think cryptic stands of willow bank

caress my name? These are the famous sayings I have time and time
again professed, my public name. Tourniquet

correct, oblong
cancellation, I died when we were parted because everything you told me.

Caring only for your answer: die
today again when nothing tells me. That totality

was your name and what you told me, dies with me.

Moon, June

Words rhyming with
words worth mocking

cruelty,
desire

hot cognate
with cold.

Bright moving darkness of his
face over me. Bluish whites.

Why wouldn't I want to give up everything

for I never
cover me in a way I never

what if you said "I never
get what I want"

and the moon answered

really came down
over you

fucked you with a moonbeam

heart
soul
love

those kinds of words
in triplicate, converge over

one, over two,

cast doubt in shadow
until cast in doubt.

Darkness of lightness
of feeling so sure

in blindness
certain

of shadow

the rightness
of wrong-

doing.
I think you would too.

You're the smartest cat I know

You make eye contact through the window when you want to come in from a frosty mudroom.

You climb up on a screen door and hang there like a bear rug when you want to come in from the sunny porch.

You eat the foods you like until you are sick, retching in the hallway, but you will not eat the foods you don't like at all—not one morsel.

You make love to your wife's best friend, make her love you, cock and eyeballs, really love you.

Then all is awry—loss of you, hole through the wall, fixed erotic absence. Hole all the way through the wall.

You can see through it.

When all is fallen around you, babies crying on the ground, beds empty, living rooms stripped, shit in corners, she opens the door for you, the window for you, the rooms and walls and roof, attic and stairwell and hall open for you.

You make eye contact through the window.

You have no friends left.

You make eye contact through the walls.

She has no friends left.

You fuck her other friend.

Homeowner

for Anna's house and land

Pissing into someone special's grave
fresh
square
rectangle

and the mourning just goes on and on—refreshing,
peristaltic,

):

a place for my mourning to go on and on
laid. I am that widow

of my love's wife. Life
laid bare. Window down flat. I can't put anything more

out there. I can't put anything

more out there! Do you hear me, now that cries
real tears in sound in rooms. And build

a rectangle frisk
the ground up

appraiser
inspector
engineer

make frozen the ground
and lay it down.

It all goes back to my transpersonal *heart*, flooded with epi-
nephrine at a sighting, false, emotionally hallucinatory, bereaved of vision
as I am, his car in back of mine, close up on mine, why is that car following
so close on mine when it is not his, moot, response completes. It's easiest to
believe

that I am dead. There is a part of me that died and it is the best part, infant,
upstart.

Code inspector, structural
engineer, he won't penetrate that
issue. It will be easy

to live here forever if I just accept my death, and live as one dead,

meeting ghosts on their own hollow
terms. Demands that I provide a fount of self-love

suggestions that it is possible to do so, "provide this for yourself, gushing
    fount, self-
replenishing in a tall cylindrical

phase." Ghost,

I can't die because of my real children. Build
sidereal into the mountain.

But nothing can distract me, really, tall glass
fuzzy rabbit
work habit
creature comfort
all that is available

and all that is real. What is also sidereal. What can distract from what was
    most

Ghost. Sick flower, sick heart, in dirt
haunt.

Warden

No ideas but in

love—moved
out of

center to model of
wave: consider it. "Relate to this": I'm quoting my love

but it can't read you, I wiped

stuff off my phone. That broken

love: still feeds, yet beats,

empirical in the
sky that moon collude

with me wrenched free of sheer
centrality

how will he find me

by the jingling of my

key.

Romance

Sometimes even now I get this feeling

riding in the back of a small truck, covered wagon, ruched aperture to night
sky, repurposed army truck, two a.m. and I'm bouncing alongside a half
dozen hitchhikers, transient, youthful, soi-disant lorry driver away from
the Calais ferry dock en route to Paris, overnight. To arrive at dawn. I'm
traveling alone and I don't speak the language, much. The ferry ride was
rough and fluorescently lit in the cargo hold where we rode. The truck is
dark and silent, jostling over ruts—no one chats. I just look out the back
the back of the truck
into dark road disappearing behind
watching it grow lighter
in my watching
my youthful
limited—only so much of it has happened

That's when it began

romance of exoskeleton
I had such a pure sensation of myself alone
before I was alone

next-to-no language
companions slept touching me
new friends and we never would
even in our youth and fecklessness
care to speak much

so I saw myself external to the night sky
and felt myself
internally so necessarily
alone forever

even now

alone in
no-language night-sky jostling aperture soi-
disant

a point on a curve brakes

fail and the truck, its passengers plowed
guardrail and ravine and all
summarily
in the wreck.

5

Dark Roads

It is truly
a dangerous mission
tragic and heroic
lone traveler

in a continuing
for now
by hand
with just the sounds

Overall, the sounds
pertain—more importantly

sound
obtains
and all is not quiet today

on these dark roads
just one extra face

and cloaked
and not saying anything

on foot—importantly—
hand follows foot
this time.

What you see here, above
the blackened trees
their tall spiny future

are the annals of a dark
blue inadequate.

This way I say
"You made it through"

a seemingly narrow passage

Only I
darkening

for years and years

and now
is it not disturbing

to ask a question
against a book

with quiet footfall
with hooded

imposter.

It was while watching Jane Eyre

that I stumbled and fell

lost *time* and *mind*
(two words I'm forbidden)

My name stitched
in the back of her dress
stone schoolhouse

Romantic tradition:

quite like a rabbit hole

a child is born with Mother and Father
and Soul

as large as anyone's
larger than the hole.

Collapse that! into what it means

I assure you it's more boring that way

Irony is the salt of life
(I'd trade it in for gold)

Portaging takes a lot of time
and that's how we are made

A morning's worth of contretemps
Japan has bigger tides

In sharing one finds extra peace
and this is what I'll say:

"Oh, boil the cabbage down, girls"
I'm on my way to work

At work I'll find my head's in use
More mountainsides en route

In view the smallest leaf, you know
measured by a glyph

your daughter's face
my daughter's face

I really mean my daughter's face.

Today Is a Good Day
to Fly (Life Begins at)

and be contemporary

at least contemporaneous

I'm really digging this blue sky
after so much rain
with my regular menstrual

cycle
my Def Jam
progesterone cream
the blow-in (in my pocket)
(ripped out)

from in-flight music magazine
"touching cloth"
like the Romantics do.
Insert jitney.

Nothing else
touching we prepare

for our descent.
(I'm 40. Do you
know what that means.
That seems like a
joke to you. I
remember my mother's

fortieth birthday
but just barely. The

contemporaneous
line I ripped
off for her handmade
card, hackneyed
and helpless
from the start.)

Ian Curtis

It's hard to show the development of an artist—
teenaged bedroom—pictorially—hard to picture
how he grows

And then to homage,
or dedicate
songs and poems

Maybe a little bit
of the process would help. Let's see

how he contrived.

There's a ruinous, ruinous—

I'll try to sing it
as I say it—

a dark period immortalized
in (ending).

Goth magic—
If I had understood it better (appreciated it)
in high school maybe I

an emotional life

An authorized biography
of (little) JA

Bad government =
personal decisions
made impersonally

the whole life story
sane and restive

adaptive

time (is) of the essence
buying old things

Louis Quinze

bedside table

Internal, all so
internal. I could

not make it real:
"Never drive faster than your angels can fly"—

porn as conversation.
No more songs about love;

Songs about Jesus!
Impersonally

Just a little walk with thee

Remains

You can't read these stones
Their ancient theme
Long shadow on the short grass
And if you could—
the interference
the interference in your
process.

"My daughter sleeps"
the news is bad
The truth is wives
outlive their
lives. Cremains: Some wealth
pertains, in private grave-
yard and its maintenance: Lord

Byron and his walking
talk. John Keats

and his talking
clock. Tick
tock. Wordsworth,
the immortal vault. My
poem.

And when I say poem

I mean this thing

I want to write and no other

You will not be so clever

as to resurrect the feathered

the tatty wings of a costumed

angel in my dining room

tatty spatial realm

room where I exist and look at things and eat them

and float nine inches above the floor

and no one else need know

and no other poet

will do

The poet will do

what the poet will do and mime

or maim the poet

meme—in fancy

venue or classroom or focus

group the wings of the poet

relax and warm and shed and oracular

shit out the window in a pile by the side of the road

and the commitment of the poet

to engage, subvert, refract, or remand

is safe in my vagina at last where it belongs.

windowless structure

*Wrongly convicted in 1990 of rape and
assault, Yusef Salaam spent 5.5 years
in jail before being exonerated.*

10 filed fingernails
imagination inviolate

7-windowed structure
pointed at the sky

7-fingered hand
the corner holds it

"I was placed in this cell
and allowed to grow spiritually"

Do you only work in extremes?

Large and small
10 and a thousand

Am I Special

I can play songs in my head
Yes I can perfectly replicate

(the) full-on
orchestral
every note
(when the lights / go down / in the city)
yet I cannot

compose, for example

and though when I was young I believed

that the fullness meant
I could recreate the sounds
I heard in my head with my mouth

I learned through painful iteration
painfully unsatisfactory

shameful the rendition

so partial
almost unrelated
the qualities are: note tone scale register vocality musicality
incapacity
painfully shy of representation
is there anyone?

who is a record player

Rhythm "and" the Human Body

But what if the song makes money?

I wait patiently for you to identify
the gender

of your partner

examine your awesome eyebrows
        while I do so

I say "I'm so sorry to hear about that" (your loss)

and watch the veins redden
and swell
in your eyeballs

she continues
the transaction

the conviction
arises
from deep feeling

Do you like the recording I
made?
(of my body)

it was just this
one time

I sang the song but it sounded
like that
forever

Sing with me.

Kindred
Airspace
Auto-Tune.

The Nightingale
(sound of music)

I had an idea
in the middle of the night

and the confidence it brings me

is ongoing

a three-way mindmeld

including The Varieties
(of that experience)
—Benjamin (self-transmission)
not James (pragmatism)

and then I sang out loud
        for the first time in ages

Another James—a signatory
a statutory

foundational
folksong
with traditional
and recurring—

"Oh soldier, kind soldier
will you marry me"—

it could almost have been a round

but for that I was alone.

My children don't want
                to hear me sing
(it is too inexact) (it does not replicate)
my husband doesn't like to hear me sing

(it is inexact and therefore embarrassing)
the sound of it brings a flush to his cheeks like nothing else
(like something else)

6

Visions of Never Being Heard from Again

I stopped by to see you but you were not home

marshland

the pure vision

my ancient lives all rising up and risen

shudder in my bed to come up against

a living religion; they get offended so easily;

blow up your hundred-foot Buddha

no problem. Entire mountainside.

Presumably it's an improvement

on whatever came before

on what was here before

ancestral crypt your daddy built; a grassy hill; a patchwork quilt;
    inadequately warming.

What are they doing here

So limpidly, eloquent in the throes
such limpid eloquence in the face of

the ending, the sudden death
the tail end
the tail between

And then there is the problem
of no privacy

no privacy in the working life
in the breasts

No nostalgia for a lifetime of worry
On a bridge with a doe

When you look at the ferns
you see double
the ferns

something for everyone to relate to:

What I find moving now
I had overlooked in the past

the father missing the mother
after 30 years in the bed together

abstemious—
a vein opened

Death.
Yeah, that has resonance for me
Does it have resonance for you?

I write with the dictionary
I must draw with crude
strokes now—I am

alone—I have been
violated—(etc.)

The Social

Nobody invited

me.

I was standing

in this very spot
in the garden, amongst
the planted and the
wild-growing

beauties

and all around me

everyone was having a better
time than me—than *I*

now standing
corrected.

Comely, utopic visions.
How does one come by these

bionic

interventions?
Nobody stands in my shoes (negation)

I guess I really am a girl
I want to talk about these feelings

if you talked to me more about your feelings
we would have sex more

commensurate

if we slept naked
we would have sex more

correlative

flower heads nodding
happy at my feet

and systemic underground
a frail coterie.

Unfailingly

All day I was subsumed into the group

Approximately nine of us, there were
several members with significantly retarded
development
functionality

Subsumed under an azure
ceiling
thatched
roof of blinding
in a good way

footstone at the foot
of the plot we scoped
a final resting place

I never wanted to leave. It was hot, even, in the sunlight of late morning
close to the source of the heat and the light
flat on our backs on the poor soil but in number
we were many

We walked there
I was silenced by the number

And when they asked me to speak
about
my unique experience
even
in the evening

overtime
I was (imposed upon).

Not one of you was there.

Poetics Department:
A Mockery

Cross-country
it doesn't get any smaller

than this
pop culvert
telescopic culvert

Are you happy?

I am only happy
sometimes.

    *

A ridiculous trip
One hopes to be redeemed

No adventure—
deserted by adventure

there must be a reason.

the left and the right of me
You go for displacement,
entering terrain

ungirded.

*

A series of firsts
the profile

ranks the compromises

Of course the rain will have already
washed the offending
away

*

Personal safety
nothing compared to

stripy hills
spatially reconstituted

pragmatism empowered
by superstition

no legacy
of iconography

*

pretty, or at
least stubborn
skip the scenic overlook

internal precision
Last Chance to Pee
an easy walk

All you can hear
is the hissing of the pods
milkweed in the
shadow of spires

The stripes of whatever happened

*

I like a big meal
with lots of different things to eat

overrun, yes,
but not infested,
no.

*

It made me sad
I did not like to see
the way he knelt there
in his chain mail

three arrows down
in him

*

More dilemma
no more dilemma
that's exactly the kind of quandary

invalid doubles
for invalid

just like Thanatos

decided you're not a bad man.
Stay at home,
and learn to be a Jew.

In The

how strange the road at five a.m.
(exactly wakes up computrix)
were it to venture
successful manumission

half-seen and trill and ululation
down dark dawn in the quickened register
a hill I know full well

in My Imagination

simpers to the bay drown plain dissolve
shatters
against black remaindered sheet
scuttling pixels making for the hills
rattling sand an ever-clearing throat

unpathway through a mind and heart
in occidental counterpart

shut up the clamshell
edutrix
infotainmentrix

plain sight lurks
sooner still
and comes and comes

and breaks the musing
heart
upon a rock

the breathing heart
upon the margin
and leaves its single-celled
metonymy
a one-note lung

deciduous in tree
clucking for the morning to arrive
knocking its heart up its throat against
the bark

of morn
an ark. Make it

stranger still.

You'd have had to have had

a dozen friends

Romanticized the dozen into

constellate
and you the consul
at the consulate

is it really as easy as all that

and almost despite myself
almost against my better judgment

it is that noble effort
to say something when the variety is impossible—impossibly

it would have to mean that there is just one thing that you really, really

and there's never been. it's always been

Maddening

more than just an exercise, certainly

Acknowledgments

Many of these poems have appeared in publications, to the editors of which the author is grateful. These publications include and are not limited to, nor are they remembered in order of importance: *BOMB*, *Prelude*, *The White Review*, *Color Treasury*, *6×6*, *The Literary Review*, *OmniVerse*, *Connotation Press*, the Academy of American Poets Poem-a-Day, more. Ugly Duckling Presse put out a chapbook in 2014 called *WARDEN*, in which all of the poems in the fourth section of this book first appeared. THANK YOU.